W9-CLM-700

FACIAL FARE

Lynn M. Stone

Rourke
Publishing LLC
Vero Beach, Florida 32964

www.rourkepublishing.com

PHOTO CREDITS: © Lloyd Luecke: page 4, 6; © Lynn Stone: title page, 5, 7, 9, 11, 13, 15, 17,19, 21; © David Dohnal: page 8; © Jeff Chevrier: page 10; © Julianna Tilton: page 12; © Oleg Kozlov: page 14; © André Maslennikov: page 16; © Jim Jurica: page 18; © Kevin Freeman: page 20

Editor: Meg Greve

Cover design by: Nicola Stratford, bdpublishing.com

Interior design by: Renee Brady

Library of Congress Cataloging-in-Publication Data

Stone, Lynn M.

  Facial fare / Lynn M. Stone.
       p. cm. -- (What animals wear)
  Includes index.
  ISBN 978-1-60472-308-3 (hardcover)
  ISBN 978-1-60472-786-9 (softcover)

  1. Face--Miscellanea--Juvenile literature. I. Title.
  QL950.5.S76 2009
  599.9'48--dc22
                                    2008012968

Printed in the USA

CG/CG

Table of Contents

Facial Fare

An animal's facial fare is whatever it happens to have on its face. The features on an animal's face are important. Many mammals have **whiskers**. Whiskers help improve their sense of touch.

Whiskers help a tiger feel objects around it, especially in dim light.

5

Antennas

Insects and snails have **antennas** on their heads. Antennas work like your ears, mouth, and eyes. Antennas help animals sense the things around them.

The male polyphemus moth's antennas are wider than the female's antennas.

Beards

Some animals have **beards** of fur or feathers. Beards may help these animals look good to their **mates**.

The emperor **tamarin** has a long, furry beard.

Bird Faces

Special feathers form circle patterns on the great gray owl's face. Those patterns help catch and send sound to the owl's hidden ears.

Owls depend on great hearing when hunting at night.

Unlike the owl, the vulture has a bare face and neck. Vultures eat dead animals, called **carrion**.

The vulture's bare skin is easy to keep clean and dry.

Some birds have fleshy growths called **caruncles** on their heads or beaks. Caruncles probably help birds attract other birds of the same kind.

The female mute swan has a smaller caruncle than the male.

15

Eyelashes

Eyelashes are short hairs along the eyelids of mammals. Eyelashes help protect eyes from dirt.

A dog's eyelashes, like yours, help protect its eyes.

17

Snakes do not have eyelashes. Some snakes do have sharp, upturned scales near their eyes.

This viper's eye scales have earned it the name eyelash viper.

The animal kingdom is full of interesting faces. Each helps an animal with its biggest job, survival!

The snow monkey's rosy, bare cheeks lighten or darken with the monkey's mood.

Glossary

antennas (an-TEN-uhz): growths on an animal's head that helps the animal to sense more about its surroundings

beards (BIHRDS): the hair or fur that grows around the jaw and cheeks of a mammal

carrion (KAYR-ee-uhn): dead animals eaten by other animals

caruncles (KAYR-uhng-kuhls): fleshy knobs or growths at the base of a bird's beak

tamarin (TAM-uh-rin): a small monkey of the South American treetops

whiskers (WISS-kurs): stiff hair that grows around the mouth of certain animals

Index

Further Reading

Gunzi, Christiane. *The Best Book of Snakes*. Kingfisher, 2006.

Souza, Dorothy. *Look What Whiskers Can Do*. Lerner, 2006.

Swanson, Diane. *Bugs Up Close*. Kids Can Press, 2007.

Websites

www.discoverymagazine.com/digger/d92dd/d9212ddb.html

www.nationalgeographic.com/ngkids/0006/senses

www.iwrc-online.org/kids/Facts/Birds/birds.htm

About the Author

Lynn M. Stone is a widely-published wildlife and domestic animal photographer and the author of more than 500 children's books. His book *Box Turtles* was chosen as an Outstanding Science Trade Book and Selectors' Choice for 2008 by the Science Committee of the National Science Teachers' Association and the Children's Book Council.